PANDEMIC!

PANDEMIC!

COVID-19
Shakes the World

SLAVOJ ŽIŽEK

Polity

All royalties from sales of this book will be
donated to Médecins Sans Frontières.

This edition published by Polity Press, 2020

First published in the United States by OR Books LLC, New York, 2020

Reprinted 2020 (twice)

9781509546107 Hardback
9781509546114 Paperback

Printed and bound by CPI Group (UK) Ltd, Croydon, CR0 4YY

For Michael Sorkin—I know he is no longer with us,
but I refuse to believe it.

CONTENTS

INTRODUCTION
NOLI ME TANGERE

"Touch me not," according to John 20:17, is what Jesus said to Mary Magdalene when she recognized him after his resurrection. How do I, an avowed Christian atheist, understand these words? First, I take them together with Christ's answer to his disciple's question as to how we will know that he is returned, resurrected. Christ says he will be there whenever there is love between his believers. He will be there not as a person to touch, but as the bond of love and solidarity between people—so, "do not touch me, touch and deal with other people in the spirit of love."

Today, however, in the midst of the coronavirus epidemic, we are all bombarded precisely by calls not to touch others but to isolate ourselves, to maintain a proper corporeal distance. What does this mean for the injunction "touch me not?" Hands cannot reach the other person; it is only from within that we can approach one another—and the window onto "within" is our eyes. These days, when you meet someone close to you (or even a stranger) and maintain a proper distance, a deep look into the other's eyes can disclose more than an intimate touch. In one of his youthful fragments, Hegel wrote:

> The beloved is not opposed to us, he is one with our own being; we see us only in him, but then again he is not a we anymore—a riddle, a miracle [*ein Wunder*], one that we cannot grasp.

It is crucial not to read these two claims as opposed, as if the beloved is partially a "we," part of myself, and partially a riddle. Is not the miracle of love that you are part of my identity precisely insofar as you remain a miracle that I cannot grasp, a riddle not only for me but also for yourself? To quote another well-known passage from young Hegel:

> The human being is this night, this empty nothing, that contains everything in its simplicity—an unending wealth of many representations, images, of which none belongs to him—or which are not present. One catches sight of this night when one looks human beings in the eye.

INTRODUCTION: *NOLI ME TANGERE*

No coronavirus can take this from us. So there is a hope that corporeal distancing will even strengthen the intensity of our link with others. It is only now, when I have to avoid many of those who are close to me, that I fully experience their presence, their importance to me.

I can already hear a cynic's laughter at this point: OK, maybe we will get such moments of spiritual proximity, but how will this help us to deal with the ongoing catastrophe? Will we learn anything from it?

Hegel wrote that the only thing we can learn from history is that we learn nothing from history, so I doubt the epidemic will make us any wiser. The only thing that is clear is that the virus will shatter the very foundations of our lives, causing not only an immense amount of suffering but also economic havoc conceivably worse than the Great Recession. There is no return to normal, the new "normal" will have to be constructed on the ruins of our old lives, or we will find ourselves in a new barbarism whose signs are already clearly discernible. It will not be enough to treat the epidemic as an unfortunate accident, to get rid of its consequences and return to the smooth functioning of the old way of doing things, with perhaps some adjustments to our healthcare arrangements. We will have to raise the key question: What is wrong with our system that we were caught unprepared by the catastrophe despite scientists warning us about it for years?

1.

WE'RE ALL IN THE SAME BOAT NOW

Li Wenliang, the doctor who first discovered the ongoing coronavirus epidemic and was censored by authorities, was an authentic hero of our time, something like the Chinese Chelsea Manning or Edward Snowden, so no wonder his death triggered widespread anger. The predictable reaction to how the Chinese state has dealt with the epidemic is best rendered by Hong Kong-based journalist Verna Yu's comment, "If China valued free speech, there would be no coronavirus crisis. Unless Chinese citizens' freedom of speech and other basic rights are respected, such crises will only happen again . . . Human rights in China may appear to have little to do with the rest of the world but as we have seen in this crisis, disaster could occur when China thwarts the freedoms of its citizens. Surely it is time the international community takes this issue more seriously."[1]

True, one can say that the whole functioning of the Chinese state apparatus runs against old Mao's motto "Trust the people!" Rather the government runs on the

---

1. https://www.theguardian.com/world/2020/feb/08/if-china-valued-free-speech-there-would-be-no-coronavirus-crisis.

premise that one should NOT trust the people: the people should be loved, protected, taken care of, controlled . . . but not trusted. This distrust is just the culmination of the same stance displayed by the Chinese authorities when they are dealing with reactions to ecological protests or problems with workers' health. Chinese authorities ever more often resort to a particular procedure: a person (an ecological activist, a Marxist student, the chief of Interpol, a religious preacher, a Hong Kong publisher, even a popular movie actress) simply disappears for a couple of weeks before they reappear in public with specific accusations raised against them, and this protracted period of silence delivers the key message: power is exerted in an impenetrable way where nothing has to be proven. Legal reasoning comes in distant second when this basic message is delivered. But the case of disappearing Marxist students is nonetheless specific: while all disappearances concern individuals whose activities can be somehow characterized as a threat to the state, the disappearing Marxist students legitimize their critical activity by a reference to the official ideology itself.

What triggered such a panicky reaction in the Party leadership was, of course, the specter of a network of self-organization emerging through direct horizontal links between groups of students and workers, and based in Marxism, with sympathy in some old party cadres and even parts of the army. Such a network directly undermines the legitimacy of the Party's rule and denounces it as an imposture. No wonder, then, that, in recent years, the government closed down many "Maoist" websites and prohibited Marxist debate groups at universities. The most dangerous thing to do today in China is to believe seriously in the state's own official ideology. China is now paying the price for such a stance:

> The coronavirus epidemic could spread to about two-thirds of the world's population if it cannot be controlled," according to Hong Kong's leading public health epidemiologist Gabriel Leung. "People needed to have faith and trust in their government while the uncertainties of the new outbreak were worked out by the scientific community," he said, "and of course when you have social media and fake news and real news all mixed in there and then zero trust, how do you fight that epidemic? You need extra trust, an extra

sense of solidarity, an extra sense of goodwill, all
of which have been completely used up.[2]

There should be more than one voice in a healthy society,
said doctor Li from his hospital bed just prior to his death,
but this urgent need for other voices to be heard does not
necessarily mean Western-style multiparty democracy, it
just demands an open space for citizens' critical reactions
to circulate. The chief argument against the idea that the
state has to control rumors to prevent panic is that this
control itself spreads distrust and thus creates even more
conspiracy theories. Only a mutual trust between ordinary people and the state can prevent this from happening.

A strong state is needed in times of epidemics since
large-scale measures like quarantines have to be per-
formed with military discipline. China was able to quarantine tens of millions of people. It seems unlikely that,
faced with the same scale of epidemic, the United States
will be able to enforce the same measures. It's not hard
to imagine that large bands of libertarians, bearing arms
and suspecting that the quarantine was a state conspiracy, would attempt to fight their way out. So would it have

2. https://www.theguardian.com/world/2020/feb/11/coronavirus-
   expert-warns-infection-could-reach-60-of-worlds-population.

been possible to prevent the outbreak with more freedom of speech, or has China been forced to sacrifice civil liberties in the province of Hubei in order to save the world? In some sense, both alternatives are true. And what makes things even worse is that there is no easy way to separate the "good" freedom of speech from the "bad" rumors. When critical voices complain that "the truth will always be treated as a rumor" by the Chinese authorities, one should add that the official media and the vast domain of digital news are already full of rumors.

A blistering example of this was provided by one of the main Russian national television networks, Channel One, which launched a regular slot devoted to coronavirus conspiracy theories on its main evening news programme, Vremya ("Time"). The style of the reporting is ambiguous, appearing to debunk the theories while leaving viewers with the impression that they contain a kernel of truth. The central message, that shadowy Western elites, and especially the US, are somehow ultimately to blame for the coronavirus epidemic is thus propagated as a doubtful rumor: it's too crazy to be true, but nonetheless, who knows . . . ?[3] The suspension of actual truth

3. https://www.bbc.com/news/world-europe-51413870.

strangely doesn't annihilate its symbolic efficiency. Plus, we must recognize that, sometimes, not telling the entire truth to the public can effectively prevent a wave of panic that could lead to more victims. At this level, the problem cannot be solved—the only way out is the mutual trust between the people and the state apparatuses, and this is what is sorely missing in China.

As the world-wide epidemic develops, we need to be aware that market mechanisms will not be enough to prevent chaos and hunger. Measures that appear to most of us today as "Communist" will have to be considered on a global level: coordination of production and distribution will have to take place outside the coordinates of the market. One should recall here the Irish potato famine in the 1840s that devastated Ireland, with millions dead or compelled to emigrate. The British state retained their trust in market mechanisms, exporting food from Ireland even when vast numbers were suffering. We must hope that a similar brutal solution is no longer acceptable today.

One can read the ongoing coronavirus epidemic as an inverted version of H. G. Wells's *The War of the Worlds* (1897). This is the story of how after Martians conquer the earth, the desperate hero-narrator discovers that all of them have been killed by an onslaught of earthly pathogens to which they had no immunity: "slain, after all man's devices had failed, by the humblest things that God, in his wisdom, has put upon this earth." It is interesting to note that, according to Wells, the plot arose from a discussion with his brother Frank about the catastrophic effect of the British on indigenous Tasmanians. What would happen, he wondered, if Martians did to Britain what the British had done to the Tasmanians? The Tasmanians, however, lacked the lethal pathogens to defeat their invaders.[4] Perhaps an epidemic which threatens to decimate humanity should be treated as Wells's story turned around: the "Martian invaders" ruthlessly exploiting and destroying life on earth are we, humanity, ourselves; and after all devices of highly developed primates to defend themselves from us have failed, we are now threatened "by the humblest things that God, in his wisdom, has put upon this earth," stupid viruses which just blindly reproduce themselves—and mutate.

We should of course analyze in detail the social conditions which made the coronavirus epidemic possible. Just think about the way, in today's interconnected world, a British person meets someone in Singapore, returns to

4. https://en.wikipedia.org/wiki/The_War_of_the_Worlds.

England, and then goes skiing to France, infecting there four others . . . The usual suspects are waiting in line to be questioned: globalization, the capitalist market, the transience of the rich. However, we should resist the temptation to treat the ongoing epidemic as something that has a deeper meaning: the cruel but just punishment of humanity for the ruthless exploitation of other forms of life on earth. If we search for such a hidden message, we remain premodern: we treat our universe as a partner in communication. Even if our very survival is threatened, there is something reassuring in the fact that we are punished, the universe (or even Somebody-out-there) is engaging with us. We matter in some profound way. The really difficult thing to accept is the fact that the ongoing epidemic is a result of natural contingency at its purest, that it just happened and hides no deeper meaning. In the larger order of things, we are just a species with no special importance.

Reacting to the threat posed by the coronavirus outbreak, Israeli prime minister Benjamin Netanyahu immediately offered help and coordination to the Palestinian authority—not out of goodness and human consideration, but for the simple fact that it is impossible to separate Jews and Palestinians there—if one group is affected, the other will inevitably also suffer. This is the reality which we should translate into politics—now is the time to drop the "America (or whoever else) First" motto. As Martin Luther King put it more than half a century ago: "We may have all come on different ships, but we're in the same boat now."

2.

WHY ARE WE TIRED ALL THE TIME?

The coronavirus epidemic confronts us with two opposed figures that prevail in our daily lives: those, like medical staff and carers, who are overworked to the point of exhaustion, and those who have nothing to do since they are forcibly or voluntarily confined to their homes. Belonging to the second category, I feel obliged to use this predicament to propose a short reflection on the different ways in which we become tired. I will ignore here the obvious paradox of enforced inactivity itself making us tired, but let me begin with Byung-Chul Han, who provided a systematic account of how and why we live in a "burnout society."[1] Here is a short resume of Byung-Chul Han's masterpiece of the same name, shamelessly but gratefully lifted from Wikipedia:

> Driven by the demand to persevere and not to fail, as well as by the ambition of efficiency, we become committers and sacrificers at the same time and enter a swirl of demarcation, self-exploitation and collapse. When production is immaterial,

1. Byung-Chul Han, *The Burnout Society*, Redwood City: Stanford UP 2015.

everyone already owns the means of production him- or herself. The neoliberal system is no longer a class system in the proper sense. It does not consist of classes that display mutual antagonism. This is what accounts for the system's stability." Han argues that subjects become self-exploiters: "Today, everyone is an *auto-exploiting labourer in his or her own enterprise*. People are now master and slave in one. Even class struggle has transformed into an *inner struggle against oneself*." The individual has become what Han calls "the achievement-subject"; the individual does not believe they are subjugated "subjects" but rather "*projects*: Always refashioning and reinventing ourselves" which "amounts to a form of compulsion and constraint—indeed, to a *more efficient kind of subjectivation and subjugation*. As a project deeming itself free of external and alien limitations, the *I* is now subjugating itself to internal limitations and self-constraints, which are taking the form of compulsive achievement and optimization.[2]

While Han offers perspicuous observations on the new mode of subjectivation from which we can learn a lot (what he discerns is today's figure of superego),

2. https://en.wikipedia.org/wiki/Byung-Chul_Han.

I nonetheless think that a couple of critical points should be made. First, limitations and constraints are definitely not only internal: new strict rules of behavior are being enforced, especially among the members of the new "intellectual" class. Just think about the Politically Correct constraints which form a special domain of the "struggle against oneself," against "incorrect" temptations. Or take the following example of a very external limitation: A couple of years ago, the filmmaker Udi Aloni organized for the Palestinian group, Jenin Freedom Theatre, to visit New York, and there was a report on the visit in *The New York Times* which nearly wasn't published. Asked to name his most recent publication for the story, Aloni cited a volume he had edited; the problem was that the word "bi-national" was in the book's subtitle. Afraid of annoying the Israeli government, the *Times* demanded that this word be deleted, otherwise the report would not appear.

Or take another, more recent example: the British Pakistani writer Kamila Shamsie wrote a novel, *Home Fire*, a successful modernized version of *Antigone*, and was awarded several international prizes for it, among them the Nelly Sachs Prize presented by the German city of Dortmund. However, when it became known that Shamsie supported BDS, she was retroactively stripped of the prize with the explanation that, when they decided to give it to her, "the members of the jury were not aware that the author has been participating in the boycott measures against the Israeli government for its Palestinian policies since 2014.[3] This is where we stand today: Peter Handke received the 2019 Nobel Prize in Literature although he openly agreed with Serb military operations in Bosnia, while supporting a peaceful protest against the West Bank politics of Israel excludes you from the winners' table.

Second, the new form of subjectivity described by Han is conditioned by the new phase of global capitalism which remains a class system with growing inequalities—struggle and antagonisms are in no way reducible to the intra-personal "struggle against oneself." There are still millions of manual workers in Third World countries, there are big differences between different kinds of immaterial workers (suffice it to mention the growing domain of those employed in "human services," like the caretakers of old people). A gap separates the top manager who owns or runs a company from a precarious worker spending

3.   https://www.middleeasteye.net/news/german-city-reverse-prize-uk-author-kamila-shamsie-over-support-bds.

days at home alone with his/her personal computer—they are definitely not both a master and a slave in the same sense.

A lot is being written about how the old Fordist assembly line way of working is replaced by a new mode of cooperative work that leaves much more space for individual creativity. However, what is effectively going on is not so much a replacement, but an outsourcing: work for Microsoft and Apple may be organized in a more cooperative fashion, but their final products are then put together in China or Indonesia in a very Fordist way—assembly line work is simply outsourced. So we get a new division of work: self-employed and self-exploited workers (described by Han) in the developed West, debilitating assembly line work in the Third World, plus the growing domain of human care workers in all its forms (caretakers, waiters . . .) where exploitation also abounds. Only the first group (self-employed, often precarious workers) fits Han's description.

Each of the three groups implies a specific mode of being tired and overworked. The assembly line work is simply debilitating in its repetitiveness—workers get desperately tired of assembling again and again the same iPhone behind a table in a Foxconn factory in a suburb of

Shanghai. In contrast to this tiredness, what makes the human-care work so weary is the very fact that they are expected to labor with empathy, to seem to care about the "objects" of their work: a kindergarten worker is paid not just to look after children but to show affection for them, the same goes for those who take care of the old or the sick. One can imagine the strain of constantly "being nice." In contrast to the first two spheres where we can at least maintain some kind of inner distance towards what we are doing (even when we are expected to treat a child nicely, we can just pretend to do so), the third sphere demands of us something which is much more tiresome. Imagine being hired to publicize or package a product in order to seduce people into buying it—even if personally one doesn't care about the product or even hates the very idea of it. One has to engage creativity quite intensely, trying to figure out original solutions, and such an effort can be much more exhausting than repetitive assembly line work. This is the specific tiredness Han is talking about.

But it is not only precarious workers laboring behind their PC screen at home who exhaust themselves through self-exploitation. Another group should be mentioned here, usually referred to by the deceptive term "creative team work."[4] These are workers who are expected to undertake entrepreneurial functions on behalf of higher management or owners. They deal "creatively" with social organization of production and with its distribution. The role of such groups is ambiguous: on the one hand, "by appropriating the entrepreneurial functions, workers deal with the social character and meaning of their work in the confined form of profitability": "The ability to organize labor and combined cooperation efficiently and economically, and to think about the socially useful character of labour, is useful for mankind and always will be."[5] However, they are doing this under the continuous subordination of capital, i.e., with the aim of making the company more efficient and profitable, and it is this tension which makes such "creative team work" so exhausting. They are held responsible for the success of the company, while their team work also involves competition among themselves and with other groups. As organizers of the work process, they are paid to perform a

4. See Stephan Siemens and Martina Frenzel, *Das unternehmerische Wir*, Hamburg: VSA Verlag 2014.
5. Eva Bockenheimer, "Where Are We Developing the Requirements for a New Society," in Victoria Fareld and Hannes Kuch, *From Marx to Hegel and Back*, London: Bloomsbury 2020, p. 209.

role that traditionally belonged to capitalists. And so, with all the worries and responsibilities of management while remaining paid workers insecure of their future, they get the worst of both worlds.

Such class divisions have acquired a new dimension in the coronavirus panic. We are bombarded by calls to work from home, in safe isolation. But which groups can do this? Precarious intellectual workers and managers who are able to cooperate through email and teleconferencing, so that even when they are quarantined their work goes on more or less smoothly. They may gain even more time to "exploit ourselves." But what about those whose work has to take place outside, in factories and fields, in stores, hospitals and public transport? Many things have to take place in the unsafe outside so that others can survive in their private quarantine . . .

And, last but not least, we should avoid the temptation to condemn strict self-discipline and dedication to work and propagate the stance of "Just take it easy!"—*Arbeit macht frei!* ("Work sets you free") is still the right motto, although it was brutally misused by the Nazis. Yes, there is hard exhaustive work for many who deal with the effects of the epidemic—but it is a meaningful work for the benefit of the community which brings its own satisfaction, not the stupid effort of trying to succeed in the market. When a medical worker gets deadly tired from working overtime, when a caregiver is exhausted by a demanding charge, they are tired in a way that is different from the exhaustion of those driven by obsessive career moves. Their tiredness is worthwhile.

3.

TOWARDS A PERFECT STORM IN EUROPE

A perfect storm takes place when a rare combination of disparate circumstances produces an event of extreme violence: in such a case, a synergy of forces releases energy much greater than the mere sum of its individual contributors. The term was popularized by Sebastian Junger's nonfiction bestseller from 1997 about a once-in-a-hundred-years combination that, in 1991, hit the northern Atlantic east of the US coast: a high pressure system from the Great Lakes produced storm winds over Sable Island off the coast of Nova Scotia that collided with Hurricane Grace coming from the Caribbean. Junger's report focuses on the crew of the fishing boat *Andrea Gail*, which disappeared among monstrous waves.

Due to its global character, the ongoing coronavirus epidemic often provokes the comment that we are now all in the same boat. But there are signs indicating that the boat called Europe comes much closer than others to the fate of *Andrea Gail*. Three storms are gathering and combining their force above Europe. The first two are not specific to Europe: the coronavirus epidemic in its direct physical impact (quarantines, suffering and death) and its economic effects which will be worse in Europe than elsewhere since the continent is already stagnating, and is also more dependent than other regions of the world on imports and exports (for instance, the car industry is the backbone of the German economy, and the export of luxury cars to China is already at a standstill.) To these two storms, we have to add now a third one which we can call the Putogan virus: the new explosion of violence in Syria between Turkey and the Assad regime (directly supported by Russia). Both sides are coldly exploiting the suffering of millions of displaced people for their own political gains.

When Turkey began to solicit thousands of immigrants to leave for Europe, organizing their transport to the Greek border, Erdogan justified this measure with pragmatic humanitarian reasons: Turkey cannot any longer support the growing number of refugees. This excuse bears witness to a breathtaking cynicism: it ignores how Turkey itself has participated in the Syrian civil war, supporting one faction against the other, and is thus heavily responsible for the flow of refugees. Now Turkey wants Europe to share the burden of refugees, i.e., to pay the price for its ruthless politics. The fake "solution" to the crisis of the Kurds in Syria—with Turkey and Russia imposing peace so that each controls its own side – is now falling apart, but Russia and Turkey remain in an ideal position to exert pressure on Europe: the two countries control the oil supply, as well as the flow of refugees, and so can use both as a means of blackmail.

The devilish dance between Erdogan and Putin, from conflict to alliance and back to conflict, should not deceive us: both extremes are part of the same geopolitical game at the expense of the Syrian people. Not only does neither side care about their suffering, they both actively exploit it. What cannot but strike the eye is the similarity between Putin and Erdogan, who evermore stand for the two versions of the same political regime, led by a composite figure that we can call Putogan.

One should avoid the game of asking who is more responsible, Erdogan or Putin, for the crisis. They are both worse and should be treated as what they are: war criminals using the suffering of millions and destroying a country to ruthlessly pursue their goals, among which is the destruction of a united Europe. Furthermore, they are now doing this in the context of a global epidemic, a time when global cooperation is more urgent than ever, using the fear this induces as a means of pursuing their military goals. In a world with a minimal sense of justice, their place should be not in presidential palaces but the International Criminal Court in the Hague.

Now we can see how the combination of three storms makes a perfect storm: a new wave of refugees organized by Turkey can have catastrophic consequences in this time of the coronavirus epidemic. Up until now, one of the few good things about the epidemic, alongside the basic fact that it has made us sharply aware of the need for global cooperation, has been that it has not been attributed to immigrants and refugees—racism was at work mostly in perceiving the threat as originating from the Oriental Other. But if the two issues get mixed together, if refugees are perceived as linked to the spread of the epidemic (and of course there is likely to be widespread infection of coronavirus among refugees given the conditions in the crowded camps they occupy), then populist racists will have their heyday: they will be able to justify their exclusion of foreigners with "scientific" medical reasons. Sympathetic policies allowing the influx of refugees could easily trigger a reaction of panic and fear. As prime minister Viktor Orban claimed in a recent speech, Hungary could effectively become the model for all Europe to follow.

TOWARDS A PERFECT STORM IN EUROPE

To prevent this catastrophe, the first thing that is required is something almost impossible: the strengthening of Europe's operational unity, especially the coordination between France and Germany. Based on this unity, Europe should then *act* to deal with the refugee crisis. In a recent TV debate, Gregor Gysi, a key figure of the German left-wing party Die Linke, gave a good answer to an anti-immigrant spokesperson who aggressively insisted that we should feel no responsibility for the poverty in Third World countries. Instead of spending money to help them, the spokesperson argued, our states should be responsible only for the welfare of their own citizens. The gist of Gysi's answer was that if we in Europe don't accept responsibility for the Third World poor and act accordingly, then they will have no choice but to come here, which is precisely what anti-immigrant sentiment is ferociously opposed to). While it is vital to all stress tolerance and solidarity towards refuges who are arriving, this line of argument that dealing with the difficulties of refuge flows is likely to be much more effective than appeals to abstract humanitarianism, appealing to generosity and guilt stemming from the undeniable fact that the cause of much suffering in the poorer nation is the result of European racism and colonization. Such a line of argument, to maintain the existing order but with a human face, is a desperate measure likely to change nothing. Much more is needed today.

4.

WELCOME TO THE VIRAL DESERT

The ongoing spread of the coronavirus epidemic has also triggered a vast epidemic of ideological viruses which were lying dormant in our societies: fake news, paranoiac conspiracy theories, explosions of racism. The well-grounded medical need for quarantines found an echo in the ideological pressure to establish clear borders and to quarantine enemies who pose a threat to our identity.

But maybe another and much more beneficent ideological virus will spread and hopefully infect us: the virus of thinking of an alternate society, a society beyond nation-state, a society that actualizes itself in the forms of global solidarity and cooperation. Speculation is widespread that coronavirus may lead to the fall of Communist rule in China, in the same way that, as Gorbachev himself admitted, the Chernobyl catastrophe was the event that triggered the end of Soviet Communism. But there is a paradox here: coronavirus will also compel us to re-invent Communism based on trust in the people and in science.

In the final scene of Quentin Tarantino's *Kill Bill: Volume 2*, Beatrix disables the evil Bill and strikes him with the "Five Point Palm Exploding Heart Technique," the deadliest blow in all of martial arts. The move consists of a combination of five strikes with one's fingertips to five different pressure points on the target's body—after the target walks away and has taken five steps, their heart explodes in their body and they fall to the floor. Such an attack is part of the martial arts mythology but is not possible in real hand-to-hand combat. In the film, after Beatrix strikes him in this way, Bill calmly makes his peace with her, takes five steps and dies.

What makes this attack so fascinating is the time between being hit and the moment of death: I can have a nice conversation as long as I sit calmly, but I am aware throughout it that the moment I start to walk my heart will explode. And isn't the idea of those who speculate on how coronavirus may lead to the fall of the Communist rule in China that the coronavirus epidemics works as some kind of social "Five Point Palm Exploding Heart Technique" on the Chinese Communist regime: the Chinese leadership can sit, observe and go through the usual motions of quarantine, but every real change in the social order (like really trusting the people) will bring their downfall. My modest opinion is much more radical: the coronavirus epidemic is a kind of "Five Point Palm Exploding Heart Technique" on the global capitalist system—a signal that we cannot go on the way we have till now, that a radical change is needed.

Years ago, Fredric Jameson drew attention to the utopian potential in movies about a cosmic catastrophe such as an asteroid threatening life on earth, or a virus wiping out humanity. Such a universal threat gives birth to global solidarity, our petty differences become insignificant, we all work together to find a solution—and here we are today, in real life. This is not a call to sadistically enjoy widespread suffering insofar as it helps our Cause—on the contrary, the point is to reflect upon the sad fact that we need a catastrophe to be able to rethink the very basic features of the society in which we live.

The first vague model of such a global coordination is the World Health Organization from which we are not getting the usual bureaucratic gibberish but precise warnings proclaimed without panic. Such organizations should be given more executive power. While US presidential candidate Bernie Sanders is mocked by skeptics for his advocacy of universal healthcare in the US, isn't the lesson of the coronavirus epidemic that even more is needed, that we should start to put together some kind of *global* healthcare network? A day after Iran's deputy health minister, Iraj Harirchi, appeared at a press conference in order to downplay the coronavirus spread and to assert that mass quarantines are not necessary, he made a short statement admitting that he has contracted the coronavirus and placed himself in isolation (even during his TV appearance, he had displayed signs of fever and weakness). Harirchi added: "This virus is democratic, and it doesn't distinguish between poor and rich or between the statesman and an ordinary citizen."[1] In this, he was deeply right—we are all in the same boat. It is difficult to miss the supreme irony of the fact that what has brought us all together and promoted global solidarity expresses itself at the level of everyday life in strict commands to avoid close contacts with others, even to self-isolate.

And we are not dealing only with viral threats—other catastrophes are looming on the horizon or already taking place: droughts, heatwaves, killer storms, the list is long. In all these cases, the answer is not panic but the hard and urgent work to establish some kind of efficient global coordination.

The first illusion to get rid of is the one floated by Donald Trump during his recent visit to India: that the epidemic will recede quickly, we just have to wait for it to

---

1. https://www.theguardian.com/world/2020/feb/25/ irans-deputy-health-minister-i-have-coronavirus.

spike and then life will return to normal. China is already preparing for this moment: their media announced that when the epidemic is over, people will have to work Saturdays and Sundays to catch up. Against these all too easy hopes, it's important to accept is that the threat is here to stay: even if this wave recedes, it will likely reappear in new, perhaps even more dangerous, forms. The fact that we already have patients who survived coronavirus infection, were proclaimed cured, and then became infected again, is an ominous sign in this direction.

For this reason, we can expect that viral epidemics will affect our most elementary interactions with other people and objects around us, including our own bodies: Instructions about how to deal with this will abound: avoid touching things which may be (invisibly) dirty, do not touch hooks, do not sit on public toilets or on benches in public places, avoid embracing others or shaking their hands . . . and be especially careful about how you control your own body and your spontaneous gestures: do not touch your nose or rub your eyes—in short, do not play with yourself. So it's not only the state and other agencies that will seek to control us, we should learn to control and discipline ourselves! Maybe only virtual reality will be considered safe, and moving freely in an open space will be reserved for the islands owned by the ultra-rich.[2]

But even here, at the level of virtual reality and the internet, we should remind ourselves that, in the last decades, the terms "virus" and "viral" were mostly used to designate digital viruses that infected our web-space and of which we were not aware, at least not until their destructive power (say, of destroying our data or our hard drive) was unleashed. What we see now is a massive return to the original literal meaning of the term: viral infections work hand in hand in both dimensions, real and virtual.

Another weird phenomenon that we can observe is the triumphant return of capitalist animism, of treating social phenomena such as markets or financial capital as living entities. If one reads our big media, the impression one gets is that what we should really worry about are not the thousands who have already died and the many more who will, but the fact that "markets are panicking"—coronavirus is ever more disturbing the smooth functioning of the world market. Does all this not clearly signal the urgent need for a reorganization of global economy which will no longer be at the mercy of market mechanisms? We

2. I owe this insight to Andreas Rosenfelder.

are not talking here about the old-style Communism, of course, just about some kind of global organization that can control and regulate the economy, as well as limit the sovereignty of nation-states when needed. Countries were able to do it in the conditions of war, and we are now effectively approaching a state of medical war.

We should not be afraid to note some potentially beneficial side effect of the epidemic. One of the lasting symbols of the epidemic is passengers trapped in quarantine on large cruise ships. Good riddance to the obscenity of such ships say I, though we have to be careful that travel to lone islands or other resorts will not once again become the exclusive privilege of the rich few, as it was decades ago with flying. Amusement parks are turning into ghost towns—perfect, I cannot imagine a more boring and stupid place than Disneyland. Car production is seriously affected—good, this may compel us to think about alternatives to our obsession with individual vehicles. The list can go on.

In a recent speech, Viktor Orban said: "There is no such thing as a liberal. A liberal is nothing more than a Communist with a diploma."[3] What if the opposite is

3. https://www.euronews.com/2020/02/16/hungary-s-orban-lashes-out-at-slow-eu-growth-sinister-menaces-and-george-soros.

true? If we designate as "liberals" those who care for our freedoms, and as "Communists" those who are aware that we can save those freedoms only with radical changes since global capitalism is approaching a crisis, then we should say that, today, those of us who still recognize ourselves as Communists, are liberals with a diploma— liberals who seriously studied why our liberal values are under threat and became aware that only a radical change can save them.

5.

THE FIVE STAGES OF EPIDEMICS

Maybe we can learn something about our reactions to the coronavirus epidemic from Elisabeth Kübler-Ross who, in her *On Death and Dying*, proposed the famous schema of the five stages of how we react upon learning that we have a terminal illness: *denial* (one simply refuses to accept the fact: "This can't be happening, not to me."); *anger* (which explodes when we can no longer deny the fact: "How can this happen to me?"); *bargaining* (the hope we can somehow postpone or diminish the fact: "Just let me live to see my children graduate."); *depression* (libidinal disinvestment: "I'm going to die, so why bother with anything?"); *acceptance* ("I can't fight it, I may as well prepare for it."). Later, Kübler-Ross applied these stages to any form of catastrophic personal loss (joblessness, death of a loved one, divorce, drug addiction), and also emphasized that they do not necessarily come in the same order, nor are all five stages experienced by all patients.

One can discern the same five stages whenever a society is confronted with some traumatic break. Let's take the threat of ecological catastrophe: first, we tend to deny it (it's just paranoia, all that's happening are the usual oscillations in weather patterns); then comes anger (at big corporations which pollute our environment, at the government which ignores the dangers); this is followed by bargaining (if we recycle our waste, we can buy some time; also there are good sides to it: we can grow vegetables in Greenland, ships will be able to transport goods from China to the US much faster on the new northern passage, new fertile land is becoming available in Siberia due to the melting of permafrost . . .), depression (it's too late, we're lost . . .); and, finally, acceptance—we are dealing with a serious threat, and we'll have to change our entire way of life!

The same holds for the growing threat of digital control over our lives: first, we tend to deny it (it's an exaggeration, a Leftist paranoia, no agency can control our daily activity); then we explode in anger (at big companies and secret state agencies who know us better than we know ourselves and use this knowledge to control and manipulate us); next, bargaining (authorities have the right to search for terrorists, but not to infringe upon our privacy . . .); followed by depression (it's too late, our privacy is lost, the time of personal freedoms is over); and, finally, acceptance (digital control is a threat to our freedom, we should render the public aware of all its dimensions and engage ourselves to fight it!).

In medieval times, the population of an affected town reacted to the signs of plague in a similar way: first denial, then anger at our sinful lives for which we are punished, or even at the cruel God who allowed it, then bargaining (it's not so bad, let's just avoid those who are ill . . .), then depression (our life is over . . .), then, interestingly, orgies (since our lives are over, let's get out of it all the pleasures still possible with lots of drinking and sex), and, finally, acceptance (here we are, let's just behave as much as possible as if normal life goes on . . .).

And is this not also how we are dealing with the coronavirus epidemic that exploded at the end of 2019? First, there was a denial (nothing serious is going on, some irresponsible individuals are just spreading panic); then, anger (usually in a racist or anti-state form: the Chinese are guilty, our state is not efficient . . .); next comes bargaining (OK, there are some victims, but it's less serious than SARS, and we can limit the damage . . .); if this doesn't work, depression arises (let's not kid ourselves, we are all doomed) . . . but how would will the final stage of acceptance look? It's a strange fact that this epidemic displays a feature common with the latest round of social protests in places like France and Hong Kong, They don't explode and then pass away, they persist, bringing permanent fear and fragility to our lives.

What we should accept and reconcile ourselves to, is that there is a sub-layer of life, the undead, stupidly repetitive, pre-sexual life of viruses, which has always been there and which will always be with us as a dark shadow, posing a threat to our very survival, exploding when we least expect it. And at an even more general level, viral epidemics remind us of the ultimate contingency and meaninglessness of our lives: no matter how magnificent the spiritual edifices we, humanity, construct, a stupid natural contingency like a virus or an asteroid can end it all . . . not to mention the lesson of ecology, which is that we, humanity, can also unknowingly contribute to this end.

6.

THE VIRUS OF IDEOLOGY

One interesting question raised by the coronavirus epidemic, even for a non-expert in statistics like me, is: where does data end and ideology begin?

There is a paradox at work here: the more our world is connected, the more a local disaster can trigger global fear and eventually a catastrophe. In the Spring of 2010, a dust cloud from a minor volcanic eruption in Iceland, a small disturbance in the complex mechanism of the life on the Earth, put to a standstill the aerial traffic over most of Europe. It was a sharp reminder of how, despite all its tremendous activity of transforming nature, humankind remains merely another of many living species on planet Earth. The very catastrophic socioeconomic impact of such a minor outburst is due to the fragility of our technological development, in this case air travel. A century ago, such an eruption would have passed unnoticed. Technological development makes us more independent from nature and at the same time, at a different level, more dependent on nature's whims. And the same holds for the spread of coronavirus: if it had happened before Deng Xiaoping's reforms, we probably wouldn't even have heard about it.

PANDEMIC!

One thing is sure: isolation alone, building new walls and further quarantines, will not do the job. Full unconditional solidarity and a globally coordinated response are needed, a new form of what was once called Communism. If we do not orient our efforts in this direction, then Wuhan today may well be typical of the city of our future. Many dystopias already imagine a similar future: we stay at home, work on our computers, communicate through videoconferences, exercise on a machine in the corner of our home office, occasionally masturbate in front of a screen displaying hardcore sex, and get food by delivery, never seeing other human beings in person.

There is, however, an unexpected emancipatory prospect hidden in this nightmarish vision. I must admit that during these last days I caught myself dreaming of visiting Wuhan. The abandoned streets in a megalopolis—the usually bustling urban centers looking like ghost towns, stores with open doors and no customers, just a lone walker or a single car here and there, provide a glimpse of what a non-consumerist world might look like. The melancholic beauty of the empty avenues of Shanghai or Hong Kong remind me of some old post-apocalyptic movies like *On the Beach*, which shows a city with most of its population wiped out—no big spectacular destruction, just the world out there no longer ready-at-hand, awaiting us, looking at us and for us. Even the white masks worn by the few people walking around provide a welcome anonymity and liberation from the social pressure of recognition.

Many of us remember the famous conclusion of the students' Situationist manifesto published in 1966: *Vivre sans temps mort, jouir sans entraves* (to live without dead time, to enjoy without obstacles). If Freud and Lacan taught us anything, it is that this formula, the supreme case of a superego injunction (since, as Lacan aptly demonstrated, superego is at its most basic a positive injunction to enjoy, not a negative act of prohibiting something) is in fact a recipe for disaster: the urge to fill in every moment of the time allotted to us with intense engagement unavoidably ends up in a suffocating monotony. Dead time—moments of withdrawal, of what old mystics called *Gelassenheit*, releasement—are crucial for the revitalization of our life experience. And, perhaps, one can hope that one of the unintended consequences of the coronavirus quarantines in cities around the world will be that some people at least will use their time released from hectic activity and think about the (non)sense of their predicament.

I am fully aware of the danger I am courting in making public these thoughts. Am I not engaging in a new version of attributing to the suffering victims some deeper authentic insight from my (as yet) safe external position and thus cynically legitimizing their suffering? When a masked citizen of Wuhan walks around searching for medicine or food, there are definitely no anti-consumerist thoughts on his or her mind, just panic, anger and fear. My plea is just that even horrible events can have unpredictable positive consequences.

Carlo Ginzburg proposed the notion that being ashamed of one's country, not love of it, may be the true mark of belonging to it. Maybe, in this time of isolation and forced quietness, some Israelis will gather the courage to feel shame in relation to the politics done on their behalf by Netanyahu and Trump—not, of course, in the sense of shame of being Jewish but, on the contrary, of feeling shame for what the Israeli politics in the West Bank is doing to the most precious legacy of Judaism itself. Maybe, some British people will gather the courage to feel shame about falling for the ideological dream that brought them Brexit. But for the people in isolation in Wuhan and around the world, it's not the time to feel ashamed and stigmatized but rather the time to gather the courage and patiently persist in their struggle. The only ones truly ashamed in China are those who publicly downplayed the epidemic while over-protecting themselves, acting like those Soviet functionaries around Chernobyl who publicly claimed there was no danger while immediately evacuating their own families, or those upper managers who publicly deny global warming but are already buying houses in New Zealand or building survival bunkers in the Rocky Mountains. Maybe, the public outrage against such double standards (which is already compelling the authorities to promise transparency) will give birth to an unintended positive side effect of this crisis.

7.

CALM DOWN AND PANIC!

Our media endlessly repeat the formula "No panic!" and then we get all the data that cannot but trigger panic. The situation resembles one I remember from my youth in a Communist country, when government officials regularly assured the public there was no reason to panic. We all took such assurances as a clear sign that they were themselves panicking.

Panic has a logic of its own. The fact that, in the United Kingdom, due to the coronavirus panic, even the toilet paper rolls disappeared from the stores reminds me of a weird incident with toilet paper from my youth in Socialist Yugoslavia. All of a sudden, a rumor started to circulate that not enough toilet paper was available. The authorities promptly issued assurances that there was enough toilet paper for normal consumption, and, surprisingly, this was not only true but people mostly even believed it was true. However, an average consumer reasoned in the following way: I know there is enough toilet paper and the rumor is false, but what if some people take this rumor seriously and, in a panic, start to buy excessive reserves of toilet paper, causing an actual shortage? So I better buy reserves myself. It is not even necessary to believe that some others take the rumor seriously—it is enough to presuppose that some others believe that there are people who take the rumor seriously—the effect is the same, namely the real lack of toilet paper in the stores. Is something similar not going on in the UK and California today?

The strange counterpart of this kind of ongoing excessive fear is the absence of panic when it would have been fully justified. In the last couple of years, after the SARS and Ebola epidemics, we were told again and again that a new much stronger epidemic was just a matter of time, that the question was not IF but WHEN. Although we were convinced of the truth of these dire predictions, we somehow didn't take them seriously and were reluctant to act and engage in serious preparations—the only place we dealt with them was in apocalyptic movies like *Contagion*.

What this contrast tells us is that panic is not a proper way to confront a real threat. When we react in panic, we do not take the threat seriously—we, on the contrary, trivialize it. Just think how ridiculous is the notion that having enough toilet paper would matter in the midst of a deadly epidemic. So what would be an appropriate reaction to the coronavirus epidemic? What should we learn and what should we do to confront it seriously?

When I suggested that the coronavirus epidemic may give a new boost of life to Communism, my claim was, as expected, ridiculed. Although it seems that the strong approach to the crisis by the Chinese state has worked—or at least worked much better than what is now occurring in Italy, the old authoritarian logic of Communists in power also clearly demonstrated its limitations. One example was the fear of bringing bad news to those in power (and to the public) that outweighed actual results—this was the reason why those who first reported on a new virus were arrested, and there are reports that a similar phenomenon is occurring now the epidemic is waning.

> The pressure to get China back to work after the coronavirus shutdown is resurrecting an old temptation: doctoring data so it shows senior officials what they want to see. This phenomenon is playing out in Zhejiang province, an industrial hub on the east coast, in the form of electricity usage. At least three cities there have given local factories targets to hit for power consumption because they're using the data to show a resurgence in production, according to people

familiar with the matter. That's prompted some businesses to run machinery even as their plants remain empty, the people said.[1]

We can also guess what will follow when those in power catch wind of this cheating: local managers will be accused of sabotage and severely punished, thus reproducing the vicious cycle of distrust. A Chinese Julian Assange is needed to expose to the public the concealment in China's response to the epidemic. But if this is not the Communism I have in mind, what do I mean by Communism? To understand it, one just has to read the public declarations of WHO. Here is a recent one:

> WHO chief Dr. Tedros Adhanom Ghebreyesus said Thursday that although public health authorities across the globe have the ability to successfully combat the spread of the virus, the organization is concerned that in some countries the level of political commitment does not match the threat level. "This is not a drill. This is not the time to give up. This is not a time for excuses. This is a time for pulling out all the stops. Countries have been planning for scenarios

1. https://www.bloomberg.com/news/articles/2020-03-01/china-s-push-to-jump-start-economy-revives-worries-of-fake-data.

like this for decades. Now is the time to act on those plans," Tedros said. "This epidemic can be pushed back, but only with a collective, coordinated and comprehensive approach that engages the entire machinery of government."[2]

One might add that such a comprehensive approach should reach well beyond the machinery of single governments: it should encompass local mobilization of people outside state control as well as strong and efficient international coordination and collaboration. If thousands become hospitalized with breathing problems, a vastly increased number of respiratory machines will be needed, and to get them, the state should directly intervene in the same way as it intervenes in conditions of war when thousands of guns are needed. It should also seek cooperation with other states. As in a military campaign, information should be shared and plans fully coordinated. This is all I mean by the "Communism" needed today, or, as Will Hutton put it:

Now, one form of unregulated, free-market globalization with its propensity for crises and pandemics is certainly dying. But another form

2. https://edition.cnn.com/2020/03/06/asia/coronavirus-covid-19-update-who-intl-hnk/index.html.

that recognizes interdependence and the primacy of evidence-based collective action is being born.

What now still predominates is the stance of "every country for itself":

> there are national bans on exports of key products such as medical supplies, with countries falling back on their own analysis of the crisis amid localized shortages and haphazard, primitive approaches to containment.[3]

The coronavirus epidemic does not signal just the limit of the market globalization, it also signals the even more fatal limit of nationalist populism which insists on full state sovereignty: it's over with "America (or whoever) first!" since America can be saved only through global coordination and collaboration. I am not a utopian here, I don't appeal to an idealized solidarity between people— on the contrary, the present crisis demonstrates clearly how global solidarity and cooperation is in the interest of the survival of all and each of us, how it is the only rational egotist thing to do. And it's not just coronavirus:

3. https://www.theguardian.com/commentisfree/2020/mar/08/the-coronavirus-outbreak-shows-us-that-no-one-can-take-on-this-enemy-alone.

China itself suffered a gigantic swine flu months ago, and it is now threatened by the prospect of a locust invasion. And, as Owen Jones has noted,[4] climate crisis is killing many more people around the world than coronavirus, but there is no panic about this.

From a cynical, vitalist standpoint, one could be tempted to see coronavirus as a beneficial infection that allows humanity to get rid of the old, weak and ill, like pulling out the half-rotten weed so that younger, healthier plants can prosper, and thus contribute to global health. The broad Communist approach I am advocating is the only way for us to leave behind such a primitive standpoint. Signs of curtailing unconditional solidarity are already discernible in the ongoing debates, as in the following note about the role of the "three wise men" if the epidemic takes a more catastrophic turn in the UK:

> NHS patients could be denied lifesaving care during a severe coronavirus outbreak in Britain if intensive care units are struggling to cope, senior doctors have warned. Under a so-called "three wise men" protocol, three senior consultants in each hospital would be forced to make decisions

4. https://www.theguardian.com/commentisfree/2020/mar/05/governments-coronavirus-urgent-climate-crisis.

on rationing care such as ventilators and beds, in the event hospitals were overwhelmed with patients.[5]

What criteria will the "three wise men" rely on? Sacrifice of the weakest and eldest? And will this situation not open up the space for immense corruption? Do such procedures not indicate that we are getting ready to enact the most brutal logic of the survival of the fittest? So, again, the choice we face is: barbarism or some kind of reinvented Communism.

5. https://www.msn.com/en-gb/news/uknews/coronavirus-weakest-patients-could-be-denied-lifesaving-care-due-to-lack-of-funding-for-nhs-doctors-admit/ar-BBl0raxq

8.
MONITOR AND PUNISH?
YES, PLEASE!

Many liberal and Leftist commentators have noted how the coronavirus epidemic serves to justify and legitimize measures of control and regulation of the people, measures that were till now unthinkable in a Western democratic society. The lockdown of all of Italy is surely a totalitarian's wildest aspiration come true. No wonder that, as matters stand now, China, with its widespread digitalized social control, proved to be best equipped for coping with a catastrophic epidemic. Does this mean that, at least in some aspects, China is our future?

The Italian philosopher Giorgio Agamben has reacted to the coronavirus epidemic in a radically different way from the majority of commentators.[1] Agamben deplored the "frantic, irrational, and absolutely unwarranted emergency measures adopted for a supposed epidemic of coronavirus" which is just another version of flu, and asked: "why do the media and the authorities do their utmost to create a climate of panic, thus provoking a true state of exception, with severe limitations on movement and

1. http://positionswebsite.org/giorgio-agamben-the-state-of-exception-provoked-by-an-unmotivated-emergency/.

the suspension of daily life and work activities for entire regions?"

Agamben sees the main reason for this "disproportionate response" in "the growing tendency to use the state of exception as a normal governing paradigm." The measures imposed in the emergency allow the government to limit seriously our freedoms by executive decree:

> It is blatantly evident that these restrictions are disproportionate to the threat from what is, according to the NRC, a normal flu, not much different from those that affect us every year. We might say that once terrorism was exhausted as a justification for exceptional measures, the invention of an epidemic could offer the ideal pretext for broadening such measures beyond any limitation." The second reason is "the state of fear, which in recent years has diffused into individual consciousnesses and which translates into a real need for states of collective panic, for which the epidemic once again offers the ideal pretext.

Agamben is describing an important aspect of the functioning of state control in the ongoing epidemic, but there are questions that remain open: why would state power be interested in promoting such a panic which is accompanied by distrust in state power ("they are helpless, they are not doing enough . . .") and which disturbs the smooth reproduction of capital? Is it really in the interest of capital and state power to trigger a global economic crisis in order to renovate its reign? Are the clear signs that state power itself, not just ordinary people, is also in panic, aware of not being able to control the situation—are these signs really just a stratagem?

Agamben's reaction is just the extreme form of a widespread Leftist stance of reading the "exaggerated panic" caused by the virus spread as a mixture of an exercise of social control combined with elements of outright racism, as when Trump refers to "the Chinese virus." However, such social interpretation doesn't make the reality of the threat disappear. Does this reality compel us to effectively curtail our freedoms? Quarantines and similar measures of course limit our freedom, and new activists following in the shoes of Chelsea Manning, Julian Assange and Edward Snowden are needed to expose their possible misuses. But the threat of viral infection has also given a tremendous boost to new forms of local and global solidarity, and it has made more starkly clear the need for control over power itself. People are right to hold state power responsible: you have the power, now show us what you can do! The challenge that faces Europe is to prove

that what China did can be done in a more transparent
and democratic way:

> China introduced measures that Western Europe
> and the USA are unlikely to tolerate, perhaps to
> their own detriment. Put bluntly, it is a mistake
> to reflexively interpret all forms of sensing and
> modelling as "surveillance" and active govern-
> ance as "social control." We need a different and
> more nuanced vocabulary of intervention.[2]

Everything hinges on this "more nuanced vocabulary":
the measures necessitated by the epidemic should not be
automatically reduced to the usual paradigm of surveil-
lance and control propagated by thinkers like Foucault.
What I fear today more than the measures applied by
China and Italy is that they apply these measures in a way
that will not work and contain the epidemic, and that the
authorities will manipulate and conceal the true data.

Both Alt-Right and fake Left refuse to accept the full
reality of the epidemic, each watering it down in an exercise of social-constructivist reduction, i.e., denouncing it
on behalf of its social meaning. Trump and his partisans
repeatedly insist that the epidemic is a plot by Democrats

2. Benjamin Bratton, personal communication.

and China to make him lose the election, while some on the Left denounce the measures proposed by the state and health apparatuses as tainted by xenophobia and therefore insist on continuing social interaction, symbolized by still shaking hands. Such a stance misses the paradox: not to shake hands and isolate when needed IS today's form of solidarity.

Who, going forward, will be able to afford to continue shaking hands and embracing? The privileged few, that's who. Boccaccio's *Decameron* is composed of stories told by a group of seven young women and three young men sheltering in a secluded villa just outside Florence to escape the plague which afflicted the city. The financial elite will similarly withdraw into secluded zones where they will amuse themselves by telling stories in the manner of *The Decameron*, while we, ordinary people, will have to live with viruses.

What I find especially annoying is how, when our media and other powerful institutions announce some closure or cancellation, they as a rule add a fixed temporal limitation, informing us, for instance, that the "schools will be closed till April 4." The big expectation is that, after the peak, which should arrive fast, things will return to normal. In this fashion, I have already been informed that a university symposium I was to participate in has just been postponed to September. The catch is that, even if life does eventually return to some semblance of normality, it will not be the same normal as the one we experienced before the outbreak. Things we were used to as part of our daily life will no longer be taken for granted, we will have to learn to live a much more fragile life with constant threats. We will have to change our entire stance to life, to our existence as living beings among other forms of life. In other words, if we understand "philosophy" as the name for our basic orientation in life, we will have to experience a true philosophical revolution.

To make this point clearer, let me quote a popular definition: viruses are "any of various infectious agents, usually ultramicroscopic, that consist of nucleic acid, either RNA or DNA, within a case of protein: they infect animals, plants, and bacteria and reproduce only within living cells: viruses are considered as being non-living chemical units or sometimes as living organisms." This oscillation between life and death is crucial: viruses are neither alive nor dead in the usual sense of these terms, they are a kind of living dead. A virus is alive in its drive to replicate, but it is a kind of zero-level life, a biological caricature not so much of death-drive as of life at its most stupid level of repetition and multiplication. However, viruses are not the elementary form of life out of which more complex developed; they are purely parasitic, they replicate themselves through infecting more developed organisms (when a virus infects us, humans, we simply serve as its copying machine). It is in this coincidence of the opposites—elementary and parasitic—that resides the mystery of viruses: they are a case of what Schelling called *"der nie aufhebbare Rest"*: a remainder of the lowest form of life that emerges as a product of malfunctioning of higher mechanisms of multiplication and continues to haunt (infect) them, a remainder that cannot ever be re-integrated into the subordinate moment of a higher level of life.

Here we encounter what Hegel calls the speculative judgment, the assertion of the identity of the highest and the lowest. Hegel's best-known example is "Spirit is a bone" from his analysis of phrenology in *Phenomenology of Spirit*, and our example should be "Spirit is a virus." Human spirit is a kind of virus that parasitizes on the human animal, exploits it for its own self-reproduction, and sometimes threatens to destroy it. And, insofar as the medium of spirit is language, we should not forget that, at its most elementary level, language is also something mechanical, a matter of rules we have to learn and follow.

Richard Dawkins has claimed that memes are "viruses of the mind," parasitic entities which "colonize" human might, using it as a means to multiply themselves—an idea whose originator was none other than Leo Tolstoy. Tolstoy is usually perceived as a much less interesting author than Dostoyevsky, a hopelessly outdated realist for whom there is basically no place in modernity, in contrast to Dostoyevsky's existential anguish. Perhaps, however, the time has come to fully rehabilitate Tolstoy, his unique theory of art and man in general, in which we find echoes of Dawkins's notion of memes. "A person is a hominid with an infected brain, host to millions of cultural symbionts, and the chief enablers of these are the symbiont systems known as languages"[3]—is this passage from Dennett not pure Tolstoy? The basic category of Tolstoy's anthropology is *infection*: a human subject is a passive empty medium infected by affect-laden cultural elements which, like contagious bacilli, spread from one to another individual. And Tolstoy goes here to the end: he does not oppose a true spiritual autonomy to this spreading of

3. Daniel C. Dennett, *Freedom Evolves*, New York: Viking, 2003, p. 173.

affective infections; he does not propose a heroic vision of educating oneself into a mature autonomous ethical subject by way of getting rid of the infectious bacilli. The only struggle is the struggle between good and bad infections: Christianity itself is an infection, although—for Tolstoy—a good one.

Maybe this is the most disturbing thing we can learn from the ongoing viral epidemic: when nature is attacking us with viruses, it is in a way returning us our own message. The message is: what you did to me, I am now doing to you.

9.

IS BARBARISM WITH A HUMAN FACE OUR FATE?

These days I sometimes catch myself wishing to contract the virus—in this way, at least the debilitating uncertainty would be over. A clear sign of my growing anxiety is how I relate to sleep. Up until a week ago I was eagerly awaiting the end of the evening when I could escape into sleep and forget about the fears of daily life. Now it's almost the opposite: I am afraid to fall asleep since nightmares haunt me and I find myself awoken in a panic. The nightmares are about the reality that awaits me.

What reality? (I owe the line of thought that follows to Alenka Zupančič.). These days we often hear that radical social changes are needed if we want to cope with the consequences of the ongoing epidemic. As this little book testifies, I myself am among those spreading this mantra. But radical changes are already taking place. The coronavirus epidemic confronts us with something previously thought to be the impossible: the world as we knew it has stopped turning, whole countries are in a lockdown, many of us are confined to our homes facing an uncertain future in which, even if most of us survive, economic mega-crisis is likely. Our reaction to all of this, what we should do, should also be the impossible—what appears impossible within the coordinates of the existing world order. The impossible happened, our world has stopped, AND impossible is what we have to do to avoid the worst, which is—what?

I don't think the biggest threat is a regression to open barbarism, to brutal survivalist violence with public disorders, panic lynching, etc. (although, with the collapse of health and some other public services, this is also possible). More than open barbarism I fear barbarism with a human face—ruthless survivalist measures enforced with regret and even sympathy, but legitimized by expert opinions. A careful observer could easily notice the tonal change in how those holding power address us: they are not just trying to project calm and confidence, they also regularly utter dire predictions: the pandemic is likely to take about two years to run its course and the virus will eventually infect 60 to 70 percent of the global population, with millions dead. In short, their true message is that we will have to curtail the cornerstone of our social ethics: the care for the old and weak. Italy has already announced that, if things get worse, those over 80 or with other serious preexisting conditions will be simply left to die. One should note how accepting such logic of the "survival of the fittest" violates even the basic principle of military ethics, which tells us that, after the battle, one should first take care of the heavily wounded even if the chance of saving them is minimal. To avoid a misunderstanding, I want to assert that I am being an utter realist here: one should prepare medicaments to enable a painless death for the terminally ill, to spare them the unnecessary suffering. But our first principle should be not to economize but to assist uncondition-ally, irrespective of costs, those who need help, to enable their survival.

So I respectfully disagree with Giorgio Agamben who sees in the ongoing crisis as a sign that

> . . . our society no longer believes in anything but bare life. It is obvious that Italians are disposed to sacrifice practically everything—the normal conditions of life, social relationships, work, even friendships, affections, and religious and political convictions—to the danger of getting sick. Bare life—and the danger of losing it—is not something that unites people, but blinds and separates them.[1]

1. https://itself.blog/2020/03/17/giorgio-agamben-clarifications/.

Things are much more ambiguous: the threat of death *does* also unite them—to maintain a corporeal distance is to show respect to the other since I also may be a virus bearer. My sons avoid me now because they are afraid they will contaminate me. What for them would likely be a passing illness can be deadly for me. If in the Cold War the rule of survival was MAD (Mutually Assured Destruction), now it is another MAD—mutually assured distance.

In the last days, we hear repeatedly that each of us is personally responsible and has to follow the new rules. Media are full of stories about people who misbehaved and put themselves and others in danger, an infected man enters a store and coughs on everyone, that sort of thing. The problem with this is the same as the journalism dealing with the environmental crisis: the media over-emphasize our personal responsibility for the problem, demanding that we pay more attention to recycling and other behavioral issues. Such a focus on individual responsibility, necessary as it is to some degree, functions as ideology the moment it serves to obfuscate the bigger questions of how to change our entire economic and social system. The struggle against coronavirus can only be fought together with the struggle against ideological mystification, and as part of a general ecological struggle. As Kate Jones put it, the transmission of disease from wildlife to humans is

> . . . a hidden cost of human economic development. There are just so many more of us, in every environment. We are going into largely undisturbed places and being exposed more and more. We are creating habitats where viruses are transmitted more easily, and then we are surprised that we have new ones.[2]

So it is not enough to put together some kind of global healthcare for humans, nature in its entirety has to be included. Viruses also attack plants, which are the main sources of our food. We have constantly to bear in mind the global picture of the world we live in, with all the paradoxes this implies. For example, it is good to know that the coronavirus lockdown in China saved more lives that the number of those killed by the virus (if one trusts official statistics):

2. https://www.theguardian.com/environment/2020/mar/18/tip-of-the-iceberg-is-our-destruction-of-nature-responsible-for-covid-19-aoe.

Environmental resource economist Marshall Burke says there is a proven link between poor air quality and premature deaths linked to breathing that air. "With this in mind," he said, "a natural—if admittedly strange—question is whether the lives saved from this reduction in pollution caused by economic disruption from COVID-19 exceeds the death toll from the virus itself." "Even under very conservative assumptions, I think the answer is a clear 'yes.'" At just two months of reduction in pollution levels he says it likely saved the lives of 4,000 children under five and 73,000 adults over 70 in China alone.[3]

We are caught in a triple crisis: medical (the epidemic itself), economic (which will hit hard whatever the outcome of the epidemic), and psychological. The basic coordinates of the everyday lives of millions are disintegrating, and the change will affect everything, from flying to holidays to simple bodily contact. We have to learn to think outside the coordinates of the stock market and profit and simply find another way to produce and

3. https://www.dailymail.co.uk/sciencetech/article-8121515/Global-air-pollution-levels-plummet-amid-coronavirus-pandemic.html.

allocate necessary resources. When the authorities learn that a company is stockpiling millions of masks, waiting for the right moment to sell them, there should be no negotiations with the company, those masks should be simply requisitioned.

The media has reported that Trump offered $1 Billion to Tübingen-based biopharmaceutical company CureVac to secure an effective coronavirus and vaccine "only for the United States." The German health minister, Jens Spahn, said a takeover of CureVac by the Trump administration was "off the table": CureVac would only develop vaccine "for the whole world, not for individual countries." Here we have an exemplary case of the struggle between privatization/barbarism and collectivism/civilization. Yet, at the same time, Trump was forced to invoke the Defense Production Act to allow the government to instruct the private sector to ramp up production of emergency medical supplies:

> Trump announces proposal to take over private sector. The US president said he would invoke a federal provision allowing the government to marshal the private sector in response to the pandemic, the Associated Press reported. Trump said he would sign an act giving himself the authority

to direct domestic industrial production "in case we need it."[4]

When I suggested recently that a way out of this crisis was a form of "Communism" I was widely mocked. But now we read, "Trump announces proposal to take over private sector." Could one even imagine such a headline prior to the epidemic? And this is just the beginning: many more measures of this sort will be needed, as well as local self-organization of communities if state-run health systems collapse under too much under stress. It is not enough just to isolate and survive—for this to be possible, basic public services will have to continue functioning: electricity and water, food and medicine will have to continue being available. We will soon need a list of those who have recovered and are, at least for some time, immune so that they can be mobilized for the urgent public work. This is not a utopian Communist vision, it is a Communism imposed by the necessities of bare survival. It is unfortunately a version of what, in the Soviet Union in 1918, was called "war Communism."

4. https://www.theguardian.com/world/2020/mar/18/coronavirus-latest-at-a-glance-wednesday-2020.

IS BARBARISM WITH A HUMAN FACE OUR FATE?

There are progressive things that only a conservative with the hard-line patriotic credentials can do: only de Gaulle was able to give independence to Algeria, only Nixon was able to establish relations with China. In both cases, if a progressive president had attempted to do these things, he would have been instantly accused of betraying the national interest. The same thing now applies with Trump limiting the freedom of private enterprises and forcing them to produce what is needed for the fight against coronavirus: if Obama were to do it, the right-wing populists would undoubtedly explode in rage, claiming that he was using the health crisis as an excuse to introduce Communism to the US.

As the saying goes: in a crisis we are all Socialists. Even Trump is now considering a form of Universal Basic Income—a check for $1,000 to every adult citizen. Trillions will be spent violating all conventional market rules. But it remains unclear how and where this will occur, and for whom? Will this enforced Socialism be the Socialism for the rich as it was with the bailing out of the banks in 2008 while millions of ordinary people lost their small savings? Will the epidemic be reduced to another chapter in the long sad story of what Naomi Klein called "disaster capitalism," or will a new better balanced, if perhaps more modest, world order emerge from it?

Everybody is saying today that we will have to change our social and economic system. But, as Thomas Piketty noted in a recent comment in *Nouvel Observateur*, what really matters is *how* we change it, in what direction, which measures are needed. A common sooth now in circulation is that, since we are all now in this crisis together, we should forget about politics and just work in unison to save ourselves. This notion is false: true politics are needed *now*—decisions about solidarity are eminently political.

10.

COMMUNISM OR BARBARISM, AS SIMPLE AS THAT!

From Alain Badiou to Byung-Chul Han[1] and many others, from the Right and the Left, I have been criticized, mocked even, after I repeatedly suggested the arrival of a form of Communism as a result of the coronavirus pandemic. The basic motifs in the cacophony of voices were easily predictable: capitalism will return in an even stronger form, using the epidemic as a disaster boost; we will all silently accept total control of our lives by the state apparatuses in the Chinese style as a medical necessity; the survivalist panic is eminently apolitical, it makes us perceive others as a deadly threat, not as comrades in a struggle. Han added some specific insights into the cultural differences between the East and the West: the developed Western countries are overreacting because they have got used to life without real enemies. Being open and tolerant, and lacking immunity mechanisms, when a real threat emerged, they were thrown into panic. But is the developed West really as permissive as it claims? Is our entire political and social space not

1. https://www.welt.de/kultur/article206681771/Byung-Chul-Han-zu-Corona-Vernunft-nicht-dem-Virus-ueberlassen.html.

permeated by apocalyptic visions: threats of ecological catastrophe, fear of Islamic refugees, panicky defense of our traditional culture against LGBT+ and gender theory? Just try to tell a dirty joke and you will immediately feel the force of Politically Correct censorship. Our permissiveness has years ago turned into its opposite.

Furthermore, does the enforced isolation really imply apolitical survivalism? I am much more in agreement with Catherine Malabou who wrote that "an *epochè*, a suspension, a bracketing of sociality, is sometimes the only access to alterity, a way to feel close to all the isolated people on Earth. Such is the reason why I am trying to be as solitary as possible in my loneliness."[2] This is a deeply Christian idea: when I feel alone, abandoned by God, at that point I am like Christ on the cross, in full solidarity with him. And, today, the same goes for Julian Assange, isolated in his prison cell, with no visits permitted. We are all now like Assange and, more than ever, we need figures like him to prevent dangerous abuses of power justified by a medical threat. In

2. https://critinq.wordpress.com/2020/03/23/to-quarantine-from-quarantine-rousseau-robinson-crusoe-and-i/?fbclid=IwAR2t6gCrl7tpdRPWhSBWXScsF54lCfRH1U-2sMEOI9PcXH7uNtKVWzKor3M.

isolation, phone and internet are our principal links with others; and both are controlled by the state who can disconnect us at its will.

So what will happen? What previously seemed impossible is already taking place: For instance on March 24, 2020 Boris Johnson announced the temporary nationalization of the UK's railways. As Assange told Yanis Varoufakis in a brief phone conversation: "this new phase of the crisis is, at the very least, making it clear to us that *anything goes*—that everything is now possible."[3] Of course, everything flows in all directions, from the best to the worst. Our situation now is therefore profoundly political: we are facing radical choices.

It is possible that, in parts of the world, state power will half-disintegrate, that local warlords will control their territories in a general *Mad Max*-style struggle for survival, especially if threats like hunger or environmental degradation accelerate. It is possible that extremist groups, will adopt the Nazi strategy of "let the old and weak die" to strengthen and rejuvenate our nation" (some groups are already encouraging members who contracted coronavirus to spread the contagion to

3. https://www.yanisvaroufakis.eu/2020/03/24/last-night-julian-assange-called-me-here-is-what-we-talked-about/.

cops and Jews, according to intelligence gathered by the FBI). A more refined capitalist version of such relapse into barbarism is already being openly debated in the US. Writing in capital letters in a tweet late on Sunday, March 22, the US president said: "WE CANNOT LET THE CURE BE WORSE THAN THE PROBLEM ITSELF. AT THE END OF THE 15-DAY PERIOD WE WILL MAKE A DECISION AS TO WHICH WAY WE WANT TO GO." Vice-President Mike Pence, who heads the White House coronavirus taskforce, said earlier on the same day that the federal Centers for Disease Control and Prevention (CDC) would issue guidance on the following Monday designed to allow people already exposed to the coronavirus to return to work sooner. And the *Wall Street Journal* editorial board warned that "federal and state officials need to start adjusting their anti-virus strategy now to avoid an economic recession that will dwarf the harm from 2008-2009." Bret Stephens, a conservative columnist at *The New York Times*, which Trump monitors closely, wrote that treating the virus as a threat comparable to the second world war "needs to be questioned aggressively before we impose solutions possibly more destructive than the virus itself."[4] Dan Patrick, the lieutenant governor of Texas, went on Fox News to argue that he would rather die than see public health measures damage the US economy, and that he believed "lots of grandparents" across the country would agree with him. "My message: let's get back to work, let's get back to living, let's be smart about it, and those of us who are 70-plus, we'll take care of ourselves."[5]

The only occasion in recent times that a similar approach was taken, as far as I know, was in the last years of Ceausescu's rule in Romania, when retired people were simply not accepted into hospitals, whatever their state, because they were no longer considered of any use to society. The message in such pronouncements is clear: the choice is between a substantial, if incalculable, number of human lives and the American (i.e. Capitalist) "way of life." In this choice, human lives lose. But is this the only choice? Are we not already, even in the US, doing something different? Of course an entire country or even the world cannot indefinitely stay in a lockdown—but it can

4. https://www.theguardian.com/world/2020/mar/23/trump-social-distancing-coronavirus-rules-guidelines-economy.
5. https://www.theguardian.com/world/2020/mar/24/older-people-would-rather-die-than-let-covid-19-lockdown-harm-us-economy-texas-official-dan-patrick.

be transformed, restarted in a new way. I have no sentimental prejudices here: who knows what we'll have to do, from mobilizing those who recovered and are immune to maintain the necessary social services, up to making available pills to enable painless death for lost cases where life is just a meaningless prolonged suffering. But we not only have a choice, we are already making choices.

This is why the stance of those who see the crisis as an apolitical moment where state power should do its task and we should just follow its instructions, hoping that some kind of normality will be restored in a not too far future, is a mistake. We should follow Immanuel Kant here who wrote with regard to the laws of the state: "Obey, but think, maintain the freedom of thought!" Today we need more than ever what Kant called the "public use of reason." It is clear that epidemics will return, combined with other ecological threats, from droughts to locusts, so hard decisions are to be made now. This is the point that those who claim this is just another epidemic with a relatively small number of dead don't get: yes, it is just an epidemic, but now we see that warnings about such epidemics in the past were fully justified, and that there is no end to them. We can of course adopt a resigned "wise" attitude of "worse things happened, think about the medieval plagues . . . " But the very need for this comparison tells a lot. The panic we are experiencing bears witness to the fact that there is some kind of ethical progress occurring, even if it is sometimes hypocritical: we are no longer ready to accept plagues as our fate.

This is where my notion of "Communism" comes in, not as an obscure dream but simply as a name for what is already going on (or at least perceived by many as a necessity), measures which are already being considered and even partially enforced. It's not a vision of a bright future but more one of "disaster Communism" as an antidote to disaster capitalism. Not only should the state assume a much more active role, organizing the production of urgently needed things like masks, test kits and respirators, sequestering hotels and other resorts, guaranteeing the minimum of survival of all new unemployed, and so on, doing all of this by abandoning market mechanisms. Just think about the millions, like those in the tourist industry, whose jobs will, for some time at least, be lost and meaningless. Their fate cannot be left to mere market mechanisms or one-off stimuluses. And let's not forget that refugees are still trying to enter Europe. It's hard to grasp their level of despair if a territory under lockdown in an epidemics is still an attractive destination for them?

Two further things are clear. The institutional health system will have to rely on the help of local communities for taking care of the weak and old. And, at the opposite end of the scale, some kind of effective international cooperation will have to be organized to produce and share resources. If states simply isolate, wars will explode. These sorts of developments are what I'm referring to when I talk about "communism," and I see no alternative to it except new barbarism. How far will it develop? I can't say, I just know that the need for it is urgently felt all around, and, as we have seen, it is being enacted by politicians like Boris Johnson, certainly no Communist.

The lines that separate us from barbarism are drawn more and more clearly. One of the signs of civilization today is the growing perception that continuing the various wars that circle the globe as totally crazy and meaningless. So too the understanding that intolerance of other races and cultures, or of sexual minorities, pales into insignificance compared with the scale of the crisis we face. This is also why, although wartime measures are needed, I find problematic the use of the term "war" for our struggle against the virus: the virus is not an enemy with plans and strategies to destroy us, it is just a stupid self-replicating mechanism.

This is what those who deplore our obsession with survival miss. Alenka Zupančič recently reread Maurice Blanchot's text from the Cold War era about the scare of nuclear self-destruction of humanity. Blanchot shows how our desperate wish to survive does not imply the stance of "forget about changes, let's just keep safe the existing state of things, let's save our bare lives." In fact the opposite is true: it is through our effort to save humanity from self-destruction that we are creating a new humanity. It is only through this mortal threat that we can envision a unified humanity.

11.

THE APPOINTMENT IN SAMARA:
A NEW USE FOR SOME OLD JOKES

On various occasions when writing previously I've recounted a joke about a man who believes himself to be a grain of seed and is taken to a mental institution, where the doctors do their best to convince him that he is not a seed but a human being. When they eventually succeed, he is allowed to leave the hospital. But he then returns immediately, trembling with fear. He reports that there is a chicken outside the entrance and he is terrified that it will eat him. "Dear fellow," says his doctor, "you know very well that you are not a seed, but a man." "Of course, I know that," replies the patient, "but does the chicken know it?"

My Croat friend Dejan Kršić recently sent me a corona-version of this joke: "Hello, my friend!" "O, hello, professor! Why are you wearing a mask? Two weeks ago you were explaining all around that masks don't protect against the virus?" "Yes, I know they don't work, but does the virus know it?"

This virus version of the joke ignores a crucial fact: the virus doesn't know anything (and also doesn't NOT know anything) because it doesn't dwell in the domain of knowledge at all, it is not an enemy trying to destroy us—it just self-reproduces with a blind automatism. Some Leftists evoke another parallel: is capital also not a virus acting as a parasite on us humans, is it also not a blind mechanism bent on expanded self-reproduction with total indifference to our suffering? There is, however, a key difference at work here: capital is a virtual entity which doesn't exist in reality independently of us; it exists only insofar as we, humans, participate in the capitalist process. As such, capital is a spectral entity: if we stop acting as if we believe in it (or, say, if a state power nationalizes all productive forces and abolishes money), capital ceases to exist, while a virus is a part of reality that can be dealt with only through science.

This does not mean that there is no link between the different levels of viral entities: biological viruses, digital viruses, capital as a viral entity. The coronavirus epidemic itself is clearly not just a biological phenomenon which affects humans: to understand its spread, one has to consider human cultural choices (such as our food habits), economy and global trade, the thick network of international relations, ideological mechanisms of fear and panic. To properly grasp this link, a new approach is needed. The path was shown by

Bruno Latour,[1] who was right to emphasize that the coronavirus crisis is a "dress rehearsal" for the forthcoming climate change which is "the next crisis, the one in which the reorientation of living conditions is going to be posed as a challenge to all of us, as will all the details of daily existence that we will have to learn to sort out carefully." The coronavirus epidemic, as a moment of the global and lasting ecological crisis, brutally imposes on us:

> . . . the sudden and painful realization that the classical definition of society—humans among themselves—makes no sense. The state of society depends at every moment on the associations between many actors, most of whom do not have human forms. This is true of microbes—as we have known since Pasteur—but also of the internet, the law, the organization of hospitals, the logistics of the state, as well as the climate.

There is, of course, as Latour is well aware, a key difference between the coronavirus epidemic and the ecological crisis:

> . . . in the health crisis, it may be true that humans as a whole are "fighting" against viruses—even if

1. Quoted from https://critinq.wordpress.com/2020/03/26/is-this-a-dress-rehearsal/.

they have no interest in us and go their way from throat to throat killing us without meaning to. The situation is tragically reversed in ecological change: this time, the pathogen whose terrible virulence has changed the living conditions of all the inhabitants of the planet is not the virus at all, it is humanity!

Although Latour immediately adds that "this does not apply to all humans, just those who make war on us without declaring war on us," the agency which "makes war on us without declaring war on us" is not just a group of people but the existing global socio-economic system—in short, the existing global order in which we all (the entirety of humanity) participate. We can see now the truly subversive potential of the notion of assemblage: it becomes apparent when we apply it to a constellation that includes humans, but can be seen from an "inhuman" standpoint, so that humans appear as just one among a variety of actants. Recall Jane Bennet's description of the way actants combine at a polluted trash site: how not only humans but also the rotting trash, worms, insects, abandoned machines, chemical poisons, and so on each play their (never purely passive) role.[2] There is an authentic theoretical and ethico-political

2. Jane Bennett, *Vibrant Matter*, Durham: Duke University Press 2010, p. 4–6.

insight in such an approach. When the so-called New Materialists like Bennett oppose the reduction of matter to a passive mixture of mechanical parts, they are, of course, not asserting the old-fashioned direct teleology, but an aleatoric dynamics immanent to matter: *emerging properties* arise out of non-predictable encounters between multiple kinds of actants, the agency for any particular act is distributed across a variety of different kinds of bodies. Agency thereby becomes a social phenomenon, where the limits of sociality are expanded to include all material bodies participating in the relevant assemblage. Say an ecological public is a group of bodies, some human, most not, that are subjected to harm, defined as a diminished capacity for action. The ethical implication of such a stance is that we should recognize our entanglement within larger assemblages: we should become more sensitive to the demands of these publics and the reformulated sense of self-interest calls upon us to respond to their plight. Materiality, usually conceived as inert substance, should be rethought as a plethora of things that form assemblages of human and nonhuman actors (actants)—humans are but one force in a potentially unbounded network of forces.

Such an approach, which locates a phenomenon in its ever-changing assemblage, enables us to account for some unexpected cases of trans-functionalization (where a phenomenon, all of a sudden, begins to function in a totally different way). Among the unexpected occurrences of solidarity, one might, for instance, look at the gangs in Rio de Janeiro that are usually engaged in brutal struggles for the control of their favelas, but who concluded peace for the duration of the coronavirus epidemic and decided to collaborate in providing help to the old and weak.[3] This sudden change was possible because street gangs were already in themselves an assemblage of different aspects: not just a form of criminal behavior, but also a form of solidarity and resistance to institutional power by groups of youth.

Another example of trans-functionalization is when the spending of trillions to help not only companies but also individuals (some such measures come close to Universal Basic Income) is justified as an extreme measure to keep the economy running and to prevent extreme poverty and starvation, but there is effectively something much more radical going on: with such measures, money no longer functions in a traditional capitalist way; it becomes a voucher to allocate available resources so that society can go on functioning, outside the constraints of the law of value.

3. I got this information from Renata Avila, a human rights lawyer from Guatemala.

Let's imagine another weird reversal along these lines. It was widely reported in our media how a collateral effect of the coronavirus epidemic was a much better quality of air above central China and now even above northern Italy. But what if weather patterns in these regions were already accustomed to polluted air, so that one of the effects of cleaner air turns out to be more destructive patterns of weather (more drought, or more flooding . . .)?

To confront the forthcoming ecological crisis, a radical philosophical change is thus needed, much more radical than the usual platitude of emphasizing how we, humans, are part of nature, just one of the natural species on Earth, i.e., of how our productive processes (our metabolism with nature, as Marx put it) is part of the metabolism within nature itself. The challenge is to describe this complex interaction in its detailed texture: coronavirus is not an exception or a disturbing intrusion, it is a particular version of a virus that was operative beneath the threshold of our perception for decades. Viruses and bacteria are ever present, sometimes even with a crucial positive function (our digestion works only through the bacteria in our stomach). It is not enough to introduce here the notion of different ontological strata (as bodies, we are organisms which act as hosts for bacteria and viruses; as producers, we collectively change the nature around us; as political beings, we organize our social life and engage in struggles in it; as spiritual beings, we find fulfilment in science, art and religion; etc.) "Assemblage" means that one has to make a step further here towards a kind of flat ontology and recognize how these different levels can interact at the same l level: viruses as actants are mediated by our productive activities, by our cultural tastes, by our social commerce. This is why, for Latour:

> Politics should become material, a *Dingpolitik* revolving around things and issues of concern, rather than around values and beliefs. Stem cells, mobile phones, genetically modified organisms, pathogens, new infrastructure and new reproductive technologies bring concerned publics into being that creates diverse forms of knowledge about these matters and diverse forms of action—beyond institutions, political interests or ideologies that delimit the traditional domain of politics.[4]

4. Martin Mueller, "Assemblages and Actor-networks: Rethinking Socio-material Power, Politics and Space," quoted from http://onlinelibrary.wiley.com/doi/10.1111/gec3.12192/pdf. It seems to me that the prevalent normative reading of Hegel a la Brandom ignores this intertwinement of normative stances and claims with a complex network of material and immaterial life-processes.

THE APPOINTMENT IN SAMARA

The coronavirus epidemic can be seen as an assemblage of a (potentially) pathogenic viral mechanism, industrialized agriculture, fast global economic development, cultural habits, exploding international communication, and so on. The epidemic is a mixture in which natural, economic and cultural processes are inextricably bound together. As an unabashed philosopher of subjectivity, I want to add two further points here: First, as humans, we are one among the actants in a complex assemblage; however, it is only and precisely as subjects that we are able to adopt the "inhuman view" from which we can (partially, at least) grasp the assemblage of actants of which we are part.

Second, "values and beliefs" should not be simply ignored: they play an important role and should be treated as a specific mode of assemblage. Religion is a complex texture of dogmas, institutions, social and individual practices, and intimate experiences where what is said and what remains unsaid is intertwined in often unexpected ways. Perhaps a full scientific proof that god exists would be of the greatest surprise for the believer her/himself. A similar complexity (or, rather, a rift) helps us to understand the belatedness of our reaction to the coronavirus spread—our knowledge was out of sync with our spontaneous beliefs.

PANDEMIC!

Recall the second murder (of the detective Arbogast) in Alfred Hitchcock's movie *Psycho*: this murder is a surprise, even more than the notorious shower scene. The stabbing in the shower is a totally unexpected surprise, while, with the detective, we know something shocking is about to happen, indeed the whole scene is shot to indicate it, but we are still surprised when it actually does. Why? How can the greatest surprise occur when what we are told will happen really occurs? The obvious answer is: because we didn't really believe it would happen. And did not something similar take place with the spread of coronavirus? Epidemiologists warned us about the virus, they actually gave quite precise predictions that have now been proven accurate. Greta Thunberg was right when she claimed that politicians should listen to science, but we were more inclined to put our trust in "hunches" (Trump used this specific word), and it is easy to understand why. What is now going on is something we until now considered impossible: the basic coordinates of our normal lives are disappearing. Our first reaction to the virus was to regard it as just a nightmare from which we would soon awaken. Now we know this will not happen, we will have to learn to live in a viral world, a new way of living will have to be painfully reconstructed.

THE APPOINTMENT IN SAMARA

But there is another combination of speech and reality at work in the ongoing pandemic: there are material processes which can happen only if they are mediated through our knowledge. We are told a specific catastrophe will happen to us, we try to avoid it, and through our very attempts to avoid it, it happens. Recall the old Arab story about the "appointment in Samara" retold by W. Somerset Maugham: a servant on an errand in the busy market of Baghdad meets Death there; terrified by its gaze, he runs home to his master and asks him to give him a horse, so that he can ride all the day and reach Samara, where Death will not find him, in the evening. The good master not only provides the servant with a horse, but goes himself to the market, looks for Death and reproaches it for scaring his faithful servant. Death replies: "But I didn't want to scare your servant. I was just surprised to see him in the market here when I have an appointment with him in Samara tonight . . . " What if the message of this story is not that a man's demise is impossible to avoid, that trying to twist free of it will only tighten its grip, but rather its exact opposite, namely that if one accepts fate as inevitable, one can break its grasp? It was foretold to Oedipus's parents that their son would kill his father and marry his mother, and the very steps they took to avoid this fate (exposing him to death in a deep forest) made sure that the prophecy would be fulfilled—without this attempt to avoid fate, fate could not have realized itself. Is this not a clear parable of the fate of the US intervention in Iraq? The US saw the signs of the fundamentalist threat, intervened to prevent it, and thereby strengthened it. Would it not have been much more effective to accept the threat, ignore it and thus break its grasp? So, back to our story: imagine that, upon encountering Death on the market, the servant addressed it thus: "What's your problem with me? If you have something you want to do to me, just do it, otherwise beat it!" Perplexed, Death would probably have mumbled something like: "But . . . we were supposed to meet in Samara, I cannot kill you here!" and run away (probably to Samara). Therein resides the wager of the so-called herd immunity coronavirus plan:

> The stated aim has been to achieve "herd immunity" in order to manage the outbreak and prevent a catastrophic "second wave" next winter [. . .]. A large proportion of the population is at lower risk of developing severe disease: roughly speaking anyone up to the age of 40. So the reasoning goes that even though in a perfect world we'd not want anyone to take the risk of infection,

> generating immunity in younger people is a way
> of protecting the population as a whole.[5]

The wager here is that, if we act as if we don't know, i.e., if we ignore the threat, the actual damage might be smaller than if we act knowingly. This is what conservative populists try to convince us of: the Samara of our appointment is our economic order and entire way of life, so that if we follow the advice of the epidemiologists and react to it by attempting to minimize the impact of the virus through isolation and lockdown, we will merely summon a catastrophe of economic collapse and poverty much more severe than the relatively small percentage of deaths from the virus.

However, as Alenka Zupančič has pointed out,[6] "let's get back to work" is an exemplary case of the deceit in Trump's apparent concern for workers: he addresses ordinary, poorly paid people for whom the pandemic is also an economic catastrophe, and who consequently cannot afford to isolate themselves. The catch here is double: First, Trump's economic policies centered around dismantling

---

5. https://www.theguardian.com/commentisfree/2020/mar/15/
   epidemiologist-britain-herd-immunity-coronavirus-covid-19.
6. Private conversation.

the welfare state are, to a large extent, responsible for the fact that many poorly paid workers find themselves in such a dire situation that, for them, poverty is a greater threat than the virus.

Second, those who will really "get back to work" are the poor, while the rich will persist in their comfortable isolation. There are those who cannot self-isolate so that the rest of us can—the healthcare workers, those responsible for producing and delivering food, those who make possible the continuing supply of electricity and water. And then there are the refugees and migrants who simply have no place they can call "home" in which to withdraw in self-isolation. How can you insist on social distancing among thousands confined to a refugee camp? Just recall the chaos in India when the government ordered a fourteen-day lockdown, with millions from the big cities trying to reach the countryside.

All these new divisions point to the fatal limitation of the Left-liberal worry that the enhanced social control triggered by the virus will continue after it has disappeared and constrain our freedom. Individuals reduced to the panic of mere survival are ideal subjects for the introduction of authoritarian power. The danger is very real: an extreme case is that of Hungarian Prime Minister

Viktor Orban, who passed a law that enables him to rule by decree for an indefinite period of time. However, this worry misses what is actually occurring today, which is almost the exact opposite: although those in power are trying to make us responsible for the outcome of the crisis, insisting that we are individually responsible for maintaining a proper distance from one another, washing our hands, wearing a mask and so on, the reality is exactly the opposite one. The message from us, the subjects, to state power is that we will gladly follow your orders, but they are YOUR orders, and there is no guarantee that our obeying them will fully work. Those in charge of the state are in a panic because they know not only that they are not in control of the situation, but also that we, their subjects, know this. The impotence of power is now laid bare.

We all know that classic scene from cartoons:[7] the cat reaches a precipice, but it goes on walking, ignoring the fact that there is no ground under its feet; it starts to fall only when it looks down and sees the abyss. When it loses its authority, the regime is like the cat above the precipice: in order to fall, it only has to be reminded to look down. But the opposite also holds true: when an authoritarian

---

7. There is probably no book of mine in which I do not refer to it at least once.

regime approaches its final crisis, its dissolution as a rule follows two steps. Before its actual collapse, a mysterious rupture takes place. All of a sudden people know that the game is over, they are no longer afraid. It is not only that the regime loses its legitimacy, its exercise of power is itself perceived as an impotent panic reaction. In his celebrated book *Shah of Shahs*, an account of the Khomeini revolution in Iran, Ryszard Kapuscinski located the precise moment of this rupture: at a Tehran crossroad, a single demonstrator refused to budge when a policeman shouted instructions at him to move, and the embarrassed policeman simply withdrew. In a couple of hours, all Tehran was talking about this incident, and although street fights continued for weeks, everyone somehow knew that the game was over . . . [8] There are indications that something similar is going on today: all the dictatorial powers that the state apparatuses are amassing simply makes their basic impotence all the more palpable.

We should resist here the temptation of celebrating this disintegration of trust as an opening for people to self-organize locally outside the state apparatuses: an efficient state which "delivers" and can be trusted, at least to some

8. See Ryszard Kapuscinski, *Shah of Shahs*, New York: Vintage Books 1992.

degree, is today needed more than ever. Self-organization of local communities can only work in combination with the state apparatus, and with science. We are now forced to admit that modern science, in spite of all its hidden biases, is the predominant form of trans-cultural universality. The epidemic provides a welcome opportunity for science to assert itself in this role.

Here, however, a new problem arises: in science also there is no big Other, no subject on which we can fully rely, who can be unequivocally presumed to know. Different epidemiologists arrive at varying conclusions, offering different proposals about what to do. Even what is presented as data is obviously filtered by horizons of pre-understanding: How, for instance, can one determine if an old, weak person really died of the virus? The fact that many more people are still dying from other diseases than from coronavirus should not be misused to alleviate the crisis, but it is true that the strict focus of our health-care system on coronavirus has led to the postponement of the treatment of diseases considered non-urgent (testing people for cancer, for liver diseases, etc.), so that our focus on corona may cause more damage in the long term that the direct impact of the virus itself. And then, of course, there are the dire economic consequences of the lockdown: by the beginning of April, local food riots of the newly impoverished had already exploded in southern Italy, with police being called in to control food stores in Palermo. Is the only choice really the one between Chinese-style near-total top-down control, and the more lax "herd immunity" approach? Hard decisions are to be made here which cannot be grounded just in scientific knowledge. It is easy to warn that state power is using the epidemic as an excuse to impose a permanent state of emergency, but what alternative arrangements do those who sound such warnings propose?

The panic that accompanies our reaction to the epidemic is not simply something orchestrated by those in power for, after all, why would big capital risk a mega-crisis of this sort? Rather, it is a genuine and well-grounded alarm. But the almost exclusive focus on the coronavirus in our media is not based on neutral facts, it clearly rests on an ideological choice. Maybe here one can perhaps allow oneself a modest conspiracy theory. What if the representatives of the existing global capitalist order are somehow aware of what critical Marxist analysts have been pointing out for some time: that the system as we know it is in deep crisis, that it cannot go on in its existing liberal-permissive form. What if these representatives are ruthlessly exploiting the epidemic in order to impose a new form of governance? The most probable outcome of the epidemic is that a new barbarian capitalism will prevail; many old and weak people will be sacrificed and left to die; workers will have to accept a much lower standard of living; digital control of our lives will remain a permanent feature; class distinctions will increasingly become a matter of life and death. How much will remain of the Communist measures that those in power are now being compelled to introduce?

So we shouldn't lose too much time in New Age spiritualist meditations on how "the virus crisis will enable us to focus on what our lives are really about." The real struggle will be over what social form will replace the liberal-capitalist New World Order. This is our true appointment in Samara.

APPENDIX
TWO HELPFUL LETTERS
FROM FRIENDS

L et me begin with a personal confession: I like the idea of being confined to one's apartment, with all the time needed to read and work. Even when I travel, I prefer to stay in a nice hotel room and ignore all the attractions of the place I'm visiting. A good essay on a famous painting means much more to me than seeing this painting in a crowded museum. But I've noticed this makes now being obliged to confine myself more difficult. To help explain this let me recount, not for the first time, the famous joke from Ernst Lubitsch's *Ninotchka*: "'Waiter! A cup of coffee without cream, please!' 'I'm sorry, sir, we have no cream, only milk, so can it be a coffee without milk?'" At the factual level, the coffee remains the same, what changes is making the coffee without cream into coffee without milk—or, more simply even, adding the implied negation and making the simple coffee into a coffee without milk. The same thing has happened to my isolation. Prior to the crisis, it was an isolation "without milk"—I could have gone out, I just chose not to. Now it's just the plain coffee of isolation with no possible negation implied.

My friend Gabriel Tupinamba, a Lacanian psychoanalyst who works in Rio de Janeiro, explained this paradox to me in an email message: "people who already worked from home are the ones who are the most anxious, and exposed to the worst fantasies of impotence, since not even a change in their habits is delimiting the singularity of this situation in their daily lives." His point is complex but clear: if there is no great change in our daily reality, then the threat is experienced as a spectral fantasy nowhere to be seen and all the more powerful for that reason. Remember that, in Nazi Germany, anti-Semitism was strongest in those parts where the number of Jews was minimal—their invisibility made them a terrifying specter.

Although self-isolated, Tupinamba continues to analyse patients via phone or skype. In his letter, he noted, with some sarcasm, how analysts who previously, for theoretical reasons, strictly opposed psychoanalytic treatment in absentia via phone or skype, immediately accepted it when directly meeting patients in person became impossible and would have meant loss of income.

Tupinamba's first reflection on the threat of coronavirus is that it brought to his mind what Freud noticed at beginning of *Beyond the Pleasure Principle*: the initial enigma that troubled Freud was that "soldiers who had been injured in the war were able to work through their traumatic experiences better than those who returned unscathed—those tended to have repeated dreams, reliving the violent imagery and fantasies from the wartime." Tupinamba links this to his memory of the famous "June Journey" political protests in Brazil in 2013:

> . . . so many of my friends from different militant organizations who were at the frontline of the protests and who got injured and beaten by the police demonstrated a sort of subjective relief of being "marked" by the situation—my intuition back then was that the bruises "scaled down" the invisible political forces shaping that moment to a manageable individual measure, giving some limits to the fantasmatic power of the state. It was as if the cuts and bruises gave the Other some contours."

("The Other" here is the all-powerful invisible agent who haunts a paranoiac.)

Tupinamba further noticed that the same paradox held during the arrival of the HIV crisis:

> . . . the invisible spread of the HIV crisis was so nerve-wracking, the impossibility of rendering ourselves commensurate with the scale of the problem, that having one's passport 'stamped' / with HIV/ did not seem, to some, like too high a price to pay for giving the situation some symbolic contours: it would at least give a measure to the power of the virus and deliver us to a situation in which, already having contracted it, we could then see what sort of freedom we would still have.

What we are dealing with here is the distinction, elaborated by Lacan, between reality and the real: reality is external reality, our social and material space to which we are used and within which we are able to orient ourselves and interact with others, while the real is a spectral entity, invisible and for that very reason appearing as all-powerful. The moment this spectral agent becomes part of our reality (even if it means catching a virus), its power is localized, it becomes something we can deal with (even if we lose the battle). As long as this transposition into reality cannot take place, "we get trapped either in anxious paranoia (pure globality) or resort to ineffective symbolisations through acting outs that expose us to unnecessary risks (pure locality)." These "ineffective symbolizations" already assumed many forms—the best known of them is Trump's call to ignore the risks and get America back to work. Such acts are much worse than shouting and clapping while watching a soccer match in front of your TV at home, acting as if you can magically influence the outcome. But this does not mean we are helpless: we can get out of this deadlock, even before science provides the technical means to constrain the virus—here is Tupinamba again:

> The fact that doctors who are in the frontline of the pandemic, people creating mutual aid systems in peripheral communities, etc., are less likely to give in to crazy paranoias, suggests to me that there is a "collateral" subjective benefit to certain forms of political work today. It seems that politics done through certain meditations—and the State is often the only available means here, but I think this might be contingent—not only provides us with the means to change the

situation, but also to give the proper form to the
things we have lost.

The fact that, in the UK, more than 400,000 young,
healthy people volunteered to help those in need as a
result of the virus, is a good sign in this direction. But
what about those among us who are not able to engage
in this way? What can we do to survive the mental pressure of living in a time of pandemic? My first rule here is:
this is not the time to search for some spiritual authen-
ticity, to confront the ultimate abyss of our being. To use
an expression by the late Jacques Lacan, try to identify
with your symptom, without any shame, which means (I
am simplifying a bit here), fully assume all small rituals,
formulas, quirks, and so on, that will help stabilize your
daily life. Everything that might work is permitted here
if it helps to avoid a mental breakdown, even forms of
fetishist denial: "I know very well . . . (how serious the
situation is), but nonetheless . . . (I don't really believe
it)." Don't think too much in the long term, just focus
on today, what you will be doing till sleep. You might
consider playing the game that features in the movie
Life is Beautiful: pretend the lockdown is just a game
that you and your family join freely and with the prospect of a big reward if you win. And, on the subject of

movies and TV, gladly succumb to all your guilty pleasures: catastrophic dystopias, comedy series with canned laughter like *Will & Grace*, YouTube documentaries on the great battles of the past. My preference is for dark Scandinavian—preferably Icelandic—crime series like *Trapped* or *Valhalla Murders*.

However, just surrendering to the screen won't fully save you. The main task is to structure your daily life in a stable and meaningful way. Here is how another of my friends, Andreas Rosenfelder, a German journalist for *Die Welt*, described the new stance towards daily life that is emerging:

> I really can feel something heroic about this new ethics, also in journalism—everybody works day and night from their home office, participating in video conferences and taking care of children or schooling them at the same time, but nobody asks why he or she is doing it, because it's not any more a question of so "I get money and can go to vacation etc.," since nobody knows if there will be vacations again and if there will be money. It's the idea of a world where you have an apartment, basics like food and water, the love of others and a task that really matters, now more than ever. The idea that one needs "more" seems unreal now.

I cannot imagine a better description of what one should shamelessly call a non-alienated, decent life, and I hope that something of this attitude will survive when the pandemic passes.

Slavoj Žižek is one of the most prolific and well-known philosophers and cultural theorists in the world today. His inventive, provocative body of work mixes Hegelian metaphysics, Lacanian psychoanalysis, and Marxist dialectic in order to challenge conventional wisdom and accepted verities on both the Left and the Right.